D1449169

GOOD FRIDAY
AND OTHER POEMS

THE MACMILLAN COMPANY
NEW YORK · BOSTON · CHICAGO · DALLAS
ATLANTA · SAN FRANCISCO

MACMILLAN & CO., LIMITED
LONDON · BOMBAY · CALCUTTA
MELBOURNE

THE MACMILLAN CO. OF CANADA, LTD.
TORONTO

GOOD FRIDAY

AND OTHER POEMS

BY

JOHN MASEFIELD

AUTHOR OF "THE EVERLASTING MERCY" "THE WIDOW
IN THE BYE STREET" "THE TRAGEDY OF
POMPEY THE GREAT," ETC.

New York
THE MACMILLAN COMPANY
1916

Norwood Press
Berwick & Smith Co., Norwood, Mass., U.S.A.

GOOD FRIDAY
A DRAMATIC POEM

PERSONS

PONTIUS PILATE, Procurator of Judæa.
PROCULA, His Wife.
LONGINUS, A Centurion.
A JEW, Leader of the Rabble.
A MADMAN.
A SENTRY.
JOSEPH OF RAMAH.
HEROD.
SOLDIERS, SERVANTS, THE JEWISH RABBLE, LOITERERS, IDLERS.

THE SCENE

The Pavement, or Paved Court, outside the Roman Citadel in Jerusalem. At the back is the barrack wall, pierced in the centre with a double bronze door, weathered to a green color.   On the right and left sides of the stage are battlemented parapets overlooking the city.   The stage or pavement is approached by stone steps from the front, and by narrow stone staircases in the wings, one on each side, well forward.   These steps are to suggest that the citadel is high up above the town, and that the main barrack gate is below. THE CHIEF CITIZEN, THE RABBLE, JOSEPH, THE MADMAN, HEROD, and THE LOITERERS, etc., enter by these steps.   PILATE, PROCULA, LONGINUS, THE SOLDIERS and SERVANTS enter by the bronze doors.

GOOD FRIDAY

A DRAMATIC POEM

PILATE. Longinus.

LONGINUS.   Lord.

PILATE [*giving scroll*]. Your warrant. Take
    the key.
Go to Barabbas' cell and set him free,
The mob has chosen him.

    LONGINUS.   And Jesus?

    PILATE.   Wait.
He can be scourged and put outside the gate,
With warning not to make more trouble here.
See that the sergeant be not too severe.
I want to spare him.

    LONGINUS.   And the Jew, the Priest,
Outside?

    PILATE. I'll see him now.

LONGINUS.   Passover Feast
Always brings trouble, Lord.   All shall be done.
Dismiss?

PILATE. Dismiss.   [*Exit* LONGINUS.
                    There's blood about the sun,
This earthquake weather presses on the brain.

Enter PROCULA.
You?

PROCULA. Dear, forgive me, if I come again
About this Jesus, but I long to know
What Herod said.   Did he dismiss him?

PILATE.   No.
He sent him back to me for me to try,
The charge being local.

PROCULA.   Have you tried him?

PILATE.   Ay,
Henceforth he will be kept outside the walls.
Now, listen, wife: whatever dream befalls,
Never again send word to me in Court
To interrupt a case.   The Jews made sport
Of what you dreamed and what you bade me fear

About this Jesus man.   The laws are clear.

I must apply them, asking nothing more

Than the proved truth.   Now tell me of your
       dream:

What was it?   Tell me then.

    PROCULA.   I saw a gleam

Reddening the world out of a blackened sky,

Then in the horror came a hurt thing's cry

Protesting to the death what no one heard.

    PILATE.   What did it say?

    PROCULA.   A cry, no spoken word

But crying, and a horror, and a sense

Of one poor man's naked intelligence,

Pitted against the world and being crushed.

Then, waking, there was noise; a rabble rushed

Following this Jesus here, crying for blood,

Like beasts half-reptile in a jungle mud.

And all the horror threatening in the dim,

In what I dreamed of, seemed to threaten
       him. . . .

So in my terror I sent word to you,

Begging you dearly to have nought to do
With that wise man.

PILATE. I grant he says wise things.
Too wise by half, and too much wisdom brings
Trouble, I find.   It disagrees with men.
We must protect him from his wisdom then.

PROCULA. What have you done to him?

PILATE.   Made it more hard
For him to wrangle in the Temple yard
Henceforth, I hope.

Enter LONGINUS.

PROCULA.   You have not punished him?

PILATE. Warned him.

LONGINUS. The envoy from the Sanhedrim
Is here, my lord.

PILATE.   Go. I must see him. Stay.
You and your women, keep within to-day.
It is the Jewish Feast and blood runs high
Against us Romans when the zealots cry
Songs of their old Deliverance through the land.
Stay, yet.   Lord Herod says that he has planned

To visit us to-night, have all prepared.

PROCULA. I would have gone to Herod had
    I dared,
To plead for this man Jesus. All shall be
Made ready. Dear, my dream oppresses me.

[Exit.

PILATE. It is this earthquake weather: it
    will end
After a shock. Farewell.

Enter CHIEF CITIZEN.

CHIEF CIT.   Hail, Lord and friend.
I come about a man in bonds with you,
One Jesus, leader of a perverse crew
That haunts the Temple.

PILATE.   Yes, the man is here.

CHIEF CIT. Charged with sedition?

PILATE.   It did not appear
That he had been seditious. It was proved
That he had mocked at rites which people loved.
No more than that. I have just dealt with him.
You wish to see him?

CH. CIT.   No, the Sanhedrim
Send me to tell you of his proved intent.
You know how, not long since, a prophet went
Through all Judæa turning people's brains
With talk of One coming to loose their chains?

PILATE. John the Baptiser whom old Herod
        killed.

CH. CIT. The Jews expect that word to be
        fulfilled,
They think that One will come.   This Jesus
        claims
To be that Man, Son of the Name of Names,
The Anointed King who will arise and seize
Israel from Rome and you.   Such claims as these
Might be held mad in other times than ours.

PILATE. He is not mad.

CH. CIT.   But when rebellion lowers
As now, from every hamlet, every farm,
One word so uttered does unreckoned harm.

PILATE. How do you know this?

CH. CIT.   From a man, his friend,

Frightened by thought of where such claims
    would end.

There had been rumors, yet we only heard

The fact but now.   We send you instant word.

    PILATE. Yes.   This is serious news.   Would I
       had known.

But none the less, this Jesus is alone.

A common country preacher, as men say,

No more than that, he leads no big array;

No one believes his claim?

    CH. CIT.   At present, no.

He had more friends a little while ago,

Before he made these claims of being King.

    PILATE. You know about him then?

    CH. CIT.   His ministering

Was known to us, of course.

    PILATE.   And disapproved?

    CH. CIT. Not wholly, no; some, truly; some
       we loved.

At first he only preached.   He preaches well.

    PILATE. What of?

CH. CIT. Of men, and of escape from hell
By good deeds done. But when he learned his
    power
And flatterers came, then, in an evil hour,
As far as I can judge, his head was turned.
A few days past, from all that we have learned
He made this claim, and since persists therein.
Deluders are best checked when they begin.
So, when we heard it from this frightened
    friend,
We took this course to bring it to an end.

PILATE. Rightly. I thank you. Do I under-
    stand
That friends have fallen from him since he
    planned
To be this King?

CH. CIT.   They have, the most part.

PILATE.   Why?
What makes them turn?

CH. CIT.   The claim is blasphemy
Punished by death under the Jewish laws.

PILATE. And under ours, if sufficient cause
Appear, and yet, if all the Jews despise
This claimant's folly, would it not be wise
To pay no heed, not make important one
Whom all contemn?

CH. CIT.   His evil is not done.
His claim persists, the rabble's mind will turn.
Better prevent him, Lord, by being stern.
The man has power.

PILATE.   That is true, he has.

CH. CIT. His is the first claim since the
        Baptist was,
Better not let it thrive.

PILATE.   It does not thrive.

CH. CIT. All ill weeds prosper, Lord, if left
        alive.
The soil is ripe for such a weed as this.
The Jews await a message such as his,
The Anointed Man, of whom our Holy Books
Prophesy much.   The Jewish people looks
For Him to come.

PILATE.   These ancient prophecies
Are drugs to keep crude souls from being wise.
Time and again Rome proves herself your
    friend,
Then some mad writing brings it to an end.
Time and again, until my heart is sick.
Dead prophets spreading madness in the quick.
And now this Jesus whom I hoped to save.
Have you the depositions?

CH. CIT.   Yes, I have.

PILATE. Give me.

CH. CIT.   This is the docquet.

PILATE.   This is grave.

CH. CIT. I thought that you would think so.

PILATE.   I will learn
What he can say to this and then return.
Wait. I must speak. Although I shall not
    spare
Anyone, man or woman, who may dare
To make a claim that threatens Roman rule,
I do not plan to be a priestly tool.

I know your Temple plots; pretend not here

That you, the priest, hold me, the Roman,
      dear.

You, like the other Jews, await this King

Who is to set you free, who is to ding

Rome down to death, as your priests' brains
      suppose.

This case of Jesus shows it, plainly shows.

He and his claim were not at once disowned;

You waited, while you thought "He shall be
      throned,

We will support him, if he wins the crowd."

You would have, too. He would have been en-
      dowed

With all your power to support his claim

Had he but pleased the rabble as at first.

But, since he will not back the priestly aim,

Nor stoop to lure the multitude, you thirst

To win my favor by denouncing him.

This rebel does not suit the Sanhedrim.

I know. . . . The next one may.

CH. CIT.   You wrong us, Sire.

PILATE. Unless he blench, you 'complish your
       desire

With Jesus, though; there is no king save Rome

Here, while I hold the reins.   Wait till I come.

                    [*Exit* PILATE.

THE MADMAN. Only a penny, a penny,

Lilies brighter than any

White lilies picked for the Feast.

He enters, tapping with his stick.

I am a poor old man who cannot see,

Will the great noble present tell to me

If this is the Paved Court?

CH. CIT.   It is.

MADMAN.   Where men

Beg for a prisoner's freedom?

CH. CIT.   Yes.   What then?

MADMAN. I come to help the choosing.

CH. CIT.   You can go.

MADMAN. Where, lord?

Ch. Cit. Why, home.   You hear that noise
     below,

Or are you deaf?

Madman.   No, lordship, only blind.

Ch. Cit. Come   this-day-next-year   if   you
     have the mind.

This year you come too late, go home again.

Madman. Lord.   Is the prisoner loosed?

Ch. Cit.   Yes, in the lane.

Can you not hear them cry "Barabbas" there?

Madman. Barabbas, Lord?

Ch. Cit.   The prisoner whom they bear

In triumph home.

Madman.   Barabbas?

Ch. Cit.   Even he.

Madman. Are not you wrong, my Lord?

Ch. Cit.   Why should I be?

Madman. There was another man in bonds,
     most kind

To me, of old, who suffer, being blind.

Surely they called for him?   One Jesus?   No?

Ch. Cit. The choice was made a little while
    ago.
Barabbas is set free, the man you name
Is not to be released.

Madman.   And yet I came
Hoping to see him loosed.

Ch. Cit.   He waits within
Till the just pain is fitted to his sin.
It will go hard with him, or I mistake.
Pray God it may.

Madman.   I sorrow for his sake.

Ch. Cit. God's scathe.

Enter more Jews.

Madman.   A penny for the love of Heaven.
A given penny is a sin forgiven.
Only a penny, friends.

1st Cit. The case was proved.   He uttered
    blasphemy.
Yet Pilate gives him stripes: the man should die.

3rd Cit. Wait here awhile.   It is not over yet.

This is the door, the man shall pay his debt.

After the beating they will let him go

And we shall catch him.

 2ND CIT.   We will treat him so

That he will not be eager to blaspheme

So glibly, soon.

 3RD CIT. We will.

 1ST CIT.   Did Pilate seem

To you, to try to spare him?

 2ND CIT.   Ay, he did,

The Roman dog.

 3RD CIT. We will not.

 2ND CIT.   God forbid.

 1ST CIT. Well, we'll stay here.

 2ND CIT. We will anoint this King.

 CH. CIT. You talk of Jesus?

 1ST CIT.   Yes.

 CH. CIT.   I had to bring

News from the Temple but a minute past,

To-day is like to be King Jesus' last.

 1ST CIT. So?

CH. CIT. It is sure.   Wait here a little while.

1ST CIT. We mean to, Lord.   His tongue
 shall not defile

Our Lord again, by God.

CH. CIT.   By a happy chance

There came a hang-dog man with looks askance,

Troubled in mind, who wished to speak with us.

He said that he had heard the man speak thus

That he was the Messiah, God in man.

He had believed this, but his doubts began

When Jesus, not content, claimed further things;

To be a yoke upon the necks of Kings,

Emperor and Priest.   Then, though he found
 him kind

In friendship, he was troubled.   With bowed
 mind

He came to us and swore what Jesus claimed.

This Emperor over Kings will now be tamed.

VOICES. Will Pilate back the priests?

CH. CIT.   He cannot fail.

It threatens Roman power.

A VOICE.   Listen, friends,

Pilate is coming; hark! the sitting ends.

No.   'Tis the Bench.

> [*The bench is set by* SLAVES.]
>
> What will Lord Pilate do?

THE SLAVES *do not answer*.

You Nubian eunuchs answer to the Jew.

Is the man cast?

A SLAVE.   The circumcised will see

When Rome is ready.

> [*Goes in and shuts the door.*]

A VOICE.   There.   They nail a tree.

They make a cross, for those are spikes being
> driven.

He's damned.

A VOICE.   Not so, he still may be forgiven.

The cross may be for one of those two thieves.

A VOICE. I had forgotten them.

A VOICE.   This man believes

That Pilate was inclined to let him go.

2ND CIT. That was before this charge came.

A VOICE.   Even so
This Roman swine is fond of swine like these.

A VOICE. Come, Pilate, come.

A VOICE.   He will not have much ease
This Paschal Feast, if Jesus is not cast.

A VOICE.   There is the door.   Lord Pilate
        comes at last.

No.   'Tis the trumpet.

                        [A TRUMPETER *comes out.*]

VOICES.   Blow the trumpet, friend.

A VOICE. Roman.   Recruit.   When will the
        sitting end?

VOICES. Fling something at him.   Roman.

A VOICE.   O, have done.
He will not hang until the midday sun
And we shall lose our sleeps.   Let sentence pass.

A VOICE [*singing*].   As I came by the market
        I heard a woman sing:

"My love did truly promise to wed me with a
        ring,

But, oh, my love deceived me and left me here
　　forlorn

With my spirit full of sorrow, and my baby to
　　be born."

A Voice. Why are you standing here?

A Voice. 　　　　　　　　　I came to see.

A Voice. O, did you so?

A Voice. 　　　　　　Why do you look at me?

A Voice. You were his friend: you come
　　from Galilee.

A Voice. I do not.

A Voice. 　　　　　Yes, you do.

A Voice. 　　　　　　　　I tell you, No.

A Voice. You know this man quite well.

A Voice. 　　　　　　　　I do not know
One thing about him.

A Voice. 　　　　　Does he know the cur?

A Voice. Ay, but denies. He was his follower.

A Voice. I was not.

A Voice. 　　　　　Why, I saw you in the hall,
I watched you.

A Voice.   I was never there at all.

A Voice. So he would be a King.

A Voice.   That was the plan.

A Voice. I swear to God I never saw the
man.

A Voice. He did; you liar; fling him down
the stair.

A Voice. I did not, friends. I hate the man,
I swear.

Voices. You swear too much for truth, down
with him, sons.

Leave him, here's Pilate.

Enter Longinus *and* Soldiers.

Longinus. Stand back. Keep further back.
Get down the stair,

Stop all this wrangling. Make less babble
there.

Keep back yet further. See you keep that line.
Silence. These Jewish pigs.

The Jews.   The Roman swine.

Enter PILATE.

PILATE. Longinus.

LONGINUS.   Lord.

PILATE. No Jew here thinks him King.
They want his blood.

LONGINUS.   They would want anything
That would beguile the hours until the Feast.

PILATE. I would be glad to disappoint the
       priest.
I like this Jesus man.   A man so wise
Ought not to end through crazy prophecies.
Still, he persists.

LONGINUS.   They are a stubborn breed.
The medicine Cross is what they mostly need.

PILATE. Still, this man is, in fact, a kind of king,
A God beside these beasts who spit and sting,
The best Jew I have known.

LONGINUS.   He had his chance.

PILATE. O, yes, he had.   We'll let the Jews
       advance
Into the court.   I tried to set him free.

Still, if he will persist, the thing must be.
And yet I am sorry.

LONGINUS.   I am sorry, too.
He seemed a good brave fellow, for a Jew.
Still, when a man is mad there is no cure
But death, like this.

PILATE.   I fear so.

LONGINUS.   I am sure.
Shall I begin?

PILATE.   Yes.

LONGINUS. Sound the Assembly. [*Trumpet.*]
          Sound
The Imperial call. [*Trumpet.*]

PILATE.   You people, gathered round,
Behold your King.

VOICES.   Our King. I see him. Where?
That heap of clothes behind the soldiers there.
He has been soundly beaten. Look, he bleeds.
A cross on Old Skull Hill is what he needs.

PILATE. What would you, then, that I should
          do to him?

VOICES. Stone the blasphemer, tear him limb
    from limb,
Kill him with stones, he uttered blasphemy,
Give him to us, for us to crucify.
Crucify!

PILATE. Would you crucify your King?

VOICES. He is no King of ours; we have no King
But Cæsar.   Crucify!

PILATE.   Bring pen and ink.

LONGINUS. Hold up the prisoner, Lucius;
    give him drink.

PILATE. I come to sentence.

SERVANT.   Writing things, my lord.

PILATE. Fasten the parchment to the piece
    of board.
So.   I will write.

VOICES.   What does his writing mean?
It is the sentence of this Nazarene,
Condemning him to death.   A little while
And he'll be ours.   See Lord Pilate smile.
Why does he smile?

PILATE.   Longinus.

LONGINUS.   Lord.

PILATE.   Come here.

Go to that man, that upland targeteer,

I want this writ in Hebrew. Bid him write

Big easy letters that will catch the sight.

    LONGINUS. I will, my lord. Make way.

                         [*Exit* LONGINUS.

    A VOICE.   What's on the scroll?

    A VOICE. It gives the prisoner into his con-
        trol

To nail to death, the foul blaspheming beast.

    A VOICE. D'you think he will be dead before
        the Feast?

    A VOICE. They'll spear him if he lingers until
        dark.

    A VOICE. When Feast begins he will be stiff
        and stark.

There's little life left in him as it is.

    VOICES. We'll hammer iron through those
        hands of his,

And through his feet, and when the cross is set
Jolt it; remember.   I will not forget.

A VOICE. Here comes the sentence.

Enter LONGINUS.

A VOICE.   Wait; it is not signed.

A VOICE. Come to the hill, you will be left
  behind.

I want a good place at the cross's foot.

A VOICE. I've got a stone for when they
  move the brute.

Besides, I mean to bait him on the way.

I'll spatter him with filth.

A VOICE.   No, come away.

PILATE. Imperial finding in the High Priest's
  suit.

In the name of Cæsar and of Rome. . . .

LONGINUS.   Salute.

PILATE. I, Procurator of Judæa, say
That Jesus, called the King, be led away
To death by crucifixion, here and now.
In the name of Cæsar and of Rome. . . .

LONGINUS.   We bow

To the sentence of the court.

PILATE.   See sentence done.

This is your warrant.

LONGINUS.   Sentence shall be done.

VOICES. Away, friends, hurry.   Keep a place
  for me.

Get there before they come, then we shall see

All of the nailing and the fixing on.

PILATE. Longinus.

LONGINUS.   Lord.

PILATE.   Display this scroll upon

The head of Jesus' cross, that men may read.

Wait; I'll declare it publicly.   Take heed. . . .

I add this word, that over Jesus' head

This scroll shall be displayed till he is dead.

Show it, Longinus.   Read it if you choose.

VOICES. "Jesus of Nazareth, the King of the
  Jews."

We'll make him King, we'll set him up in
  state.

At Golgotha. Come; drag him through the gate.

Give him his cross.   Come, soldiers.

 Ch. Cit.   Israel, wait.

Wait. I must speak. Lord Pilate.

 Voices.   Stand aside. . . .

Are we to miss his being crucified?

 Ch. Cit. Wait. Only wait. One word.

 Madman.   Lord Pilate. Lord.

 Sentry. Stand back.

 Madman.   I'll speak.

 Sentry. I'll tame you with the sword.

 Madman. Lord Pilate, Jesus is an upright
  man,

I heard his teaching since it first began.

You are mistaken, Lord, you are misled.

Spare him, great King.

 Sentry.   Get down.

 Madman.   Kill me instead.

He never said this thing.   [*He is beaten aside.*]

 Longinus.   The company,

Attention. Front. Take up the prisoner. By

The left, quick wheel.   Down to the courtyard,
    wheel.

      THE TROOPS *go out by the doors, into*
    the barracks, so as to reach the main gate
    from within.   The PRISONER *is not shown,*
    but only suggested.

  A VOICE.   He cannot lift his cross, I saw him
    reel.

  A VOICE.   We'll find a man to bring it.
    Hurry, friends.

Three to be nailed.

  A VOICE.   The thieves will make good ends;
They always do.   This fellow will die soon.

  A VOICE.   The troops will spear them all be-
    fore full moon.

Come; watch them march them out.

                   Get mud to fling.

  They hurry down the staircase O.P. side.

  CH. CIT. [*to Pilate*].   Lord Pilate, do not
    write "Jesus the King,"

But that "He called himself, 'Jesus the King.'"

PILATE. Empty this water here.

[SERVANT *does.*]

Remove this board.

Take in the bench.

CH. CIT.   I have to ask, my lord,

That you will change the wording of your scroll,

My lord, it cuts my people to the soul.

PILATE. Tell Caius Scirrus that I want him.

[*Exit* SERVANT.

So. [*To* CHIEF CITIZEN.]

What I have written, I have written. Go.

> *Exit* CHIEF CITIZEN. PILATE *watches*
> *him. A yell below as the* TROOPS *march*
> *out from the main gate.* LONGINUS' *voice*
> *is heard shouting.*

LONGINUS. Right wheel. Quick march.

Close up. Keep your files close.

> *A march is played, oboe and trumpet.*
> PILATE *goes in, the* TROOPS *salute, the*
> *bronze doors are closed, but a* SENTRY *stands*
> *outside them.* THE MADMAN *remains.*

MADMAN. They cut my face, there's blood
          upon my brow.
So, let it run, I am an old man now,
An old, blind beggar picking filth for bread.
Once I wore silk, drank wine,
Spent gold on women, feasted, all was mine;
But this uneasy current in my head
Burst, one full moon, and cleansed me, then I saw
Truth like a perfect crystal, life its flaw,
I told the world, but I was mad, they said.

I had a valley farm above a brook,
My sheep bells there were sweet,
And in the summer heat
My mill wheels turned, yet all these things they
          took;
Ah, and I gave them, all things I forsook
But that green blade of wheat,
My own soul's courage, that they did not take.

I will go on, although my old heart ache.
Not long, not long.

Soon I shall pass behind

This changing veil to that which does not
      change,

My tired feet will range

In some green valley of eternal mind

Where Truth is daily like the water's song.

Enter the CHIEF CITIZEN.

CH. CIT. Where is Lord Pilate?

MADMAN.   Gone within.

CH. CIT.   You heard

The way he spoke to me?

MADMAN.   No, not a word.

The dogs so bayed for blood, I could not hear.

Ask the tall sentry yonder with the spear.

CH. CIT. I wish to see Lord Pilate.

SENTRY.   Stand aside.

CH. CIT. Send word to him; I cannot be
      denied.

I have to see him; it concerns the State

Urgently, too, I tell you.

SENTRY.   It can wait.

CH. CIT. It may mean bloodshed.

SENTRY.   Bloodshed is my trade.

A sentry's orders have to be obeyed

The same as God's, that you were talking of.

CH. CIT. I tell you, I must see him.

SENTRY.   That's enough.

You cannot now.

MADMAN.   The soldier's words are true.

CH. CIT. Could you send word?

SENTRY.   Sir, I have answered you.

CH. CIT. Those words that Pilate wrote, the
    Hebrew screed,

May cause a riot.

MADMAN.   Yes?

CH. CIT.   And death.

SENTRY.   Indeed.

You got the poor man's life, what would you
    more?

CH. CIT. Means to see Pilate.

SENTRY.   As I said before,

You cannot. Stand away. A man like you
Ought to know better than to lead a crew
To yell for a man's blood. God stop my breath,
What does a man like you with blood and death?
Go to.

   Ch. Cit. You will not send?

   Sentry.   I will not send.

   Ch. Cit. [*going*]. You shall regret this.

   Sentry.   Right. Goodbye, my friend.

   Ch. Cit. Means will be found.

                           [*Exit.*

   Sentry. These priests, these preaching folk.

                [*Pause. Sings.*]

"Upon a summer morning, I bade my love
      goodbye,
In the old green glen so far away,
To go to be a soldier on biscuits made of rye."

It is darker than it was.

   Madman.   It is falling dark.

   Sentry. It feels like earthquake weather.
     Listen.

MADMAN.   Hark.

SENTRY. It sounded like a shock inside the
    walls.

MADMAN. God celebrates the madman's
    funerals.

SENTRY. The shouts came from the Temple.

MADMAN.   Yes, they sing
Glory to God there, having killed their King.

SENTRY. You knew that man they are hang-
    ing?

MADMAN.   Yes.   Did you?

SENTRY. Not till I saw him scourged.   Was he
    a Jew?

MADMAN. No.   Wisdom comes from God,
    and he was wise.

I have touched wisdom since they took my eyes.

SENTRY. So you were blinded?   Why?

MADMAN.   Thinking aloud,
One Passover.

SENTRY.   How so?

MADMAN.   I told the crowd

That only a bloody God would care for blood.

The crowd kill kids and smear the lintel wood,

To honor God, who lives in the pure stars.

    SENTRY. You must have suffered; they are
          angry scars.

    MADMAN. There is no scar inside.

    SENTRY.   That may be so;

Still, it was mad; men do not wish to know

The truth about their customs, nor aught else.

                            [Cries off.]

    MADMAN. They have nailed the teacher Jesus
          by those yells.

    SENTRY. It is darker. There'll be earthquake
          before night.

What sort of man was he?

    MADMAN.   He knew the right

And followed her, a stony road, to this.

    SENTRY. I find sufficient trouble in what is

Without my seeking what is right or wrong.

    MADMAN. All have to seek her, and the
          search is long.

SENTRY. Maybe.

MADMAN.   And hard.

SENTRY.   Maybe.

[*Pause. Sings.*]

"I mean to be a captain before I do return,

Though the winters they may freeze and the
summers they may burn,

I mean to be a captain and command a hundred
men

And the women who . . ."   [*A bugle call off.*]
There is recall.

The doors are opened and the SENTRY *goes.*

MADMAN. The wild-duck, stringing through
the sky,

Are south away.

Their green necks glitter as they fly,

The lake is gray,

So still, so lone, the fowler never heeds.

The wind goes rustle, rustle, through the
reeds.

*   *   *   *   *   *

There they find peace to have their own wild
    souls.

In that still lake,

Only the moonrise or the wind controls

The way they take,

Through the gray reeds, the cocking moorhen's
    lair,

Rippling the pool, or over leagues of air.

   *   *   *   *   *   *

Not thus, not thus are the wild souls of men.

No peace for those

Who step beyond the blindness of the pen

To where the skies unclose.

For them the spitting mob, the cross, the crown
    of thorns,

The bull gone mad, the saviour on his horns.

   *   *   *   *   *   *

    Beauty and Peace have made

    No peace, no still retreat,

    No solace, none.

    Only the unafraid

    Before life's roaring street

Touch Beauty's feet,

Know Truth, do as God bade,

Become God's son.   [*Pause.*]

Darkness come down, cover a brave man's pain.

Let the bright soul go back to God again.

Cover that tortured flesh, it only serves

To hold that thing which other power nerves.

Darkness, come down, let it be midnight here,

In the dark night the untroubled soul sings clear.

[*It darkens.*]

I have been scourged, blinded and crucified,

My blood burns on the stones of every street

In every town; wherever people meet

I have been hounded down, in anguish died.

[*It darkens.*]

The creaking door of flesh rolls slowly back.

Nerve by red nerve the links of living crack,

Loosing the soul to tread another track.

Beyond the pain, beyond the broken clay,

A glimmering country lies

Where life is being wise,

All of the beauty seen by truthful eyes

Are lilies there, growing beside the way.

Those golden ones will loose the torted hands,

Smooth the scarred brow, gather the breaking
        soul,

Whose earthly moments drop like falling sands

To leave the spirit whole.

Now darkness is upon the face of the earth.

                              [He goes.

  [PILATE *entering, as the darkness reddens to a*
    glare.]

    PILATE. This monstrous day is in the pangs
    of birth.

There was a shock. I wish the troops were
    back

From Golgotha. The heavens are more black

Than in the great shock in my first year's rule.

Please God these zealot pilgrims will keep cool

Nor think this done by God for any cause.

The lightning jags the heaven in bloody scraws

Like chronicles of judgment.   Now it breaks.
Now rain.

PROCULA [*entering*].   O Pilate.

PILATE.   What?

PROCULA.   For all our sakes
Speak.   Where is Jesus?

PILATE.   He is crucified.

PROCULA. Crucified?

PILATE.   Put to death.   My wife, I tried
To save him, but such men cannot be saved.
Truth to himself till death was all he craved.
He has his will.

PROCULA.   So what they said is true.
O God, my God.   But when I spoke to you
You said that you had warned him.

PILATE.   That is so.
Another charge was brought some hours ago,
That he was claiming to be that great King
Foretold by prophets, who shall free the Jews.
This he persisted in.   I could not choose
But end a zealot claiming such a thing.

PROCULA. He was no zealot.

PILATE.   Yes, on this one point.
Had he recanted, well. But he was firm.
So he was cast.

PROCULA.   The gouts of gore anoint
That temple to the service of the worm.
It is a desecration of our power.
A rude poor man who pitted his pure sense
Against what holds the world its little hour,
Blind force and fraud, priests' mummery and
        pretence,
Could you not see that this is what he did?

PILATE. Most clearly, wife. But Roman laws
        forbid
That I should weigh, like God, the worth of souls.
I act for Rome, and Rome is better rid
Of these rare spirits whom no law controls.
He broke a statute, knowing from the first
Whither his act would lead, he was not blind.

PROCULA. No, friend, he followed hungry and
        athirst

The lonely exaltation of his mind.

So Rome, our mother, profits by his death,

You think so?

PILATE.   Ay.

PROCULA.   We draw securer breath,

We Romans, from his gasping on the cross?

PILATE. Some few will be the calmer for his

loss.

Many, perhaps; he made a dangerous claim.

Even had I spared it would have been the same

A year, or two, from now.   Forget him, friend.

PROCULA. I have no part nor parcel in his end.

Rather than have it thought I buy my ease,

My body's safety, honor, dignities,

Life and the rest at such a price of pain

There [*she stabs her arm with her dagger*] is my

blood, to wash away the stain.

There.   There once more.   It fetched too dear a

price.

O God, receive that soul in paradise.

PILATE. What have you done?

PROCULA.   No matter; it atones.

His blood will clamor from the city stones.

PILATE. Go in.   No, let me bind it.

PROCULA.   Someone comes.

A councillor, I think.   Ask what he wants.

Enter JOSEPH.

JOSEPH. Greetings, Lord Pilate.

PILATE.   And to you.

JOSEPH [*to* PROCULA].   And you.

            [*to* PILATE]. I have a boon to ask.

PROCULA.   What can we do?

JOSEPH. Lord Pilate, may I speak?

PILATE [*to* PROCULA]. Go in. [*She goes in.*]
        Go on [*to* JOSEPH].

JOSEPH. The man called Christ, the follower
        of John,

Was crucified to-day by your decree.

[PILATE *bows.*] He was my master, very dear
        to me.

I will not speak of that.   I only crave

Leave to prepare his body for the grave,
And then to bury him.   May I have leave?

    PILATE. Yes, you may have him when the
        guards give leave.

Wait.   In a case like this, men may believe
That the dead master is not really dead.
This preaching man, this King, has been the
        head
Of men who may be good and mean no harm,
Whose tenets, none the less, have caused alarm
First to the priests, and through the priests to
        me.
I wish this preacher's followers to see
That teaching of the kind is to be curbed.
I mean, established truths may be disturbed,
But not the Jews, nor Rome.   You understand?

    JOSEPH. I follow; yes.

    PILATE.   A riot might be fanned,
Such things have been, over the martyr's grave.

    JOSEPH. His broken corpse is all his followers
        crave.

PILATE. Why, very well then.

JOSEPH.   Will you give your seal?

PILATE. My seal?   What for?

JOSEPH.   That I may show the guard
And have the body.

PILATE.   Gladly; but I feel . . .
Not yet; not until dark.

JOSEPH.   It will be hard
To bury him to-night . . . the feast begins.

PILATE. I know, but still, when men are
    crucified . . .

JOSEPH. There is no hope of that.   The man
    has died.

PILATE. Died?   Dead already?

JOSEPH.   Yes.

PILATE.   'Tis passing soon.

JOSEPH. God broke that bright soul's body
    as a boon.

He died at the ninth hour.

PILATE.   Are you sure?

JOSEPH. I saw him, Lord.

PILATE.   I thought he would endure
Longer than that; he had a constant mind.

JOSEPH. The great soul burns the body to a
        rind.

PILATE. But dead, already; strange. [*Calling.*]
                        You in the court,
Send me Longinus here with his report.

A VOICE. I will, my lord.

PILATE.   This teacher was your friend?

JOSEPH. Was, is, and will be, till the great
        world end;
Which God grant may be soon.

PILATE.   I disagree
With teachers of new truth. For men like me
There is but one religion, which is Rome.
No easy one to practise, far from home.
You come from Ramah?

JOSEPH.   Yes.

PILATE.   What chance is there
Of olives being good?

JOSEPH.   They should be fair.

PILATE. You will not use Italian presses? No?

JOSEPH. Man likes his own, my lord, however
    slow;

What the land made, we say, it ought to use.

PILATE. Your presses waste; oil is too good
    to lose.

But I shall not persuade.

SERVANT.   Longinus, Lord.

PILATE. Make   your   report,   centurion.
    Where's your sword?

What makes you come thus jangled? Are you
    ill?

LONGINUS. There was a shock of earthquake
    up the hill.

I have been shaken. I had meant to come

Before; but I was whirled . . . was stricken
    dumb.

I left my sword within. . . .

PILATE.   Leave it. Attend.

Is the man, Jesus, dead? This is his friend

Who wants to bury him, he says he is.

LONGINUS. Jesus is out of all his miseries.

Yes, he is dead, my lord.

PILATE.   Already?

LONGINUS.   Yes.

The men who suffer most endure the less.

He died without our help.

JOSEPH.   Then may I have

His body, Lord, to lay it in the grave?

PILATE. A sentry's there?

LONGINUS.   Yes, Lord.

PILATE.   Have you a scroll?

[*Takes paper.*]   Right.   Now some wax. [*Writes.*]

                              Give into his control

The body of the teacher; see it laid

Inside the tomb and see the doorway made

Secure with stones and sealed, then bring me
        word.

This privilege of burial is conferred

On the conditions I have named to you.

See you observe them strictly.

JOSEPH.   I will do

All that himself would ask to show my sense
Of this last kindness.   I shall go from hence
Soon, perhaps far; I give you thanks, my lord.
Now the last joy the niggard fates afford;
One little service more, and then an end
Of that divineness touched at through our
    friend.

                                [*Exit.*

  PILATE. See that the tomb is sealed by dark
    to-night.
Where were you hurt, Longinus?   You are
    white.
What happened at the cross?

  LONGINUS.   We nailed him there
Aloft, between the thieves, in the bright air.
The rabble and the readers mocked with oaths,
The hangman's squad were dicing for his
    clothes.
The two thieves jeered at him.   Then it grew
    dark,
Till the noon sun was dwindled to a spark,

And one by one the mocking mouths fell still.
We were alone on the accursed hill
And we were still, not even the dice clicked,
Only the heavy blood-gouts dropped and ticked
On to the stone; the hill is all bald stone.
And now and then the hangers gave a groan.
Up in the dark, three shapes with arms out-
    spread.
The blood-drops spat to show how slow they
    bled.
They rose up black against the ghastly sky,
God, Lord, it is a slow way to make die
A man, a strong man, who can beget men.
Then there would come another groan, and then
One of those thieves (tough cameleers those
    two)
Would curse the teacher from lips bitten through
And the other bid him let the teacher be.
I have stood much, but this thing daunted me,
The dark, the livid light, and long long groans
One on another, coming from their bones.

And it got darker and a glare began

Like the sky burning up above the man.

The hangman's squad stood easy on their spears

And the air moaned, and women were in tears,

While still between his groans the robber cursed.

The sky was grim: it seemed about to burst.

Hours had passed: they seemed like awful days.

Then . . . what was that?

   PILATE.   What? Where?

   LONGINUS.   A kind of blaze,

Fire descending.

   PILATE.   No.

   LONGINUS.   I saw it.

   PILATE.   Yes?

What was it that you saw?

   LONGINUS.   A fiery tress

Making red letters all across the heaven.

Lord Pilate, pray to God we be forgiven.

   PILATE. "The sky was grim," you said, there
      at the cross.

What happened next?

LONGINUS.   The towers bent like moss

Under the fiery figures from the sky.

Horses were in the air, there came a cry.

Jesus was calling God: it struck us dumb.

One said "He is calling God. Wait. Will God
    come?

Wait." And we listened in the glare. O sir,

He was God's son, that man, that minister,

For as he called, fire tore the sky in two,

The sick earth shook and tossed the cross askew,

The earthquake ran like thunder, the earth's
    bones

Broke, the graves opened, there were falling
    stones.

    PILATE. I felt the shock even here. Só?

    LONGINUS.   Jesus cried

Once more and drooped, I saw that he had died.

Lord, in the earthquake God had come for him.

The thought of 't shakes me sick, my eyes are
    dim.

    PILATE. Tell Scirrus to relieve you.

LONGINUS.   Lord. . . .

PILATE.   Dismiss.

Lie down and try to sleep; forget all this.

Tell Scirrus I command it. Rest to-night.

Go in, Longinus, go.

LONGINUS.   Thank you, Lord Pilate.

                         [*Exit* LONGINUS.

PILATE [*alone*]. No man can stand an earth-
    quake. Men can bear

Tumults of water and of fire and air,

But not of earth, man's grave and standing
    ground;

When that begins to heave the will goes
    round.

Longinus, too. [*Noise below*.] Listen.

                  Does Herod come?

I heard his fifes.

    The doors open. SERVANTS *enter.*

SERVANT.   Lord Herod is at hand;

Will it please your Lordship robe?

PILATE.   Sprinkle fresh sand,

For blood was shed to-day, here, under foot.

[*He robes.*]

Well, that; the other clasp.   [*Music off.*]

A VOICE.   Cohort.   Salute.

PILATE. Leave torches at the door.   Dismiss.

[SERVANTS *go.*

He comes

Welcomed by everyone; the city hums

With joy when Herod passes.   Ah, not thus

Do I go through the town.   They welcome us

With looks of hate, with mutterings, curses,

stones.

Enter PROCULA.

Come, stand with me.   Welcome Lord Herod

here.

Welcome must make amends for barrack cheer.

THE NUBIANS *hold torches at the door.*

HEROD *enters.*

Come in, good welcome, Herod.

PROCULA.   Welcome, sir.

HEROD. To Rome, to Pilate, and to Beauty,
 greeting;

Give me your hands. What joy is in this meeting.

Pilate, again. You, you have hurt your hand?

 PILATE. It is nothing, sir.

 HEROD.   Beauty has touched this land,

A wound has followed.

 PROCULA.   What you please to call

Beauty, my lord, did nothing of the kind.

An earthen vessel tilted with a wall.

 HEROD. May it soon mend. Now let me
  speak my mind.

Pilate, since you have ruled here, there have
 been

Moments of . . . discord, shall we say? between

Your government and mine. I am afraid

That I, the native here, have seldom made

Efforts for friendship with you.

 PILATE.   Come.

HEROD.   I should
Have done more than I have, done all I could,
Healed the raw wound between the land and
    Rome,
Helped you to make this hellish town a home,
Not left it, as I fear it has been, hell
To you and yours cooped in a citadel
Above rebellion brewing. For the past
I offer deep regret, grief that will last,
And shame; your generous mind leaves me
    ashamed.

    PILATE. Really, my lord.

    PROCULA.   These things must not be
    named.

    PILATE. It is generous of you to speak like
    this,
But, Herod, hark.

    PROCULA.   If things have been amiss,
The fault was ours.

    HEROD.   No, the fault was mine.
Your generous act this morning was a sign

Of scrupulous justice done to me by you
For all these years, unnoticed hitherto,
Unrecognized, unthanked. I thank you now.
Give me your hand . . . so . . . thus.

    PILATE.   Herod, I bow
To what you say. To think that I have done
Something (I know not what) that has begun
A kindlier bond between us, touches home.
I have long grieved lest I have injured Rome
By failing towards yourself, where other men
Might have been wiser. . . . That is over, then?
Our differences henceforth may be discussed
In friendly talk together;

    HEROD.   So I trust.

    PILATE. Give me your hand; I have long
        hoped for this.
I need your help, and you, perhaps, need mine.
The tribes are restless on the border-line,
The whole land seethes: the news from Rome
        is bad.
But this atones.

PROCULA.   O, fully.

HEROD.   I am glad.

PILATE. Let us go in.

HEROD.   You lead.

PROCULA.   A moment, one. . . .

You named a generous act that he had
    done. . . . ?

HEROD. This morning, yes; you sent that man
    to me

Because his crime was laid in Galilee.

A little thing, but still it touched me close;

It made me think how our disputes arose

When thieves out of your province brought to
    me

Were punished with a fine, perhaps set free,

Not sent to you to judge, as you sent him.

In future you will find me more a friend.

Or so I hope.

PILATE.   Thanks.   May the gods so send

That this may lead to happier days for us.

VOICES OF THE CROWD [*who are now flocking*

in, among them THE MADMAN]. Herod
the good, Herod the glorious.

Long life to Herod.

PILATE.   Come, the crowd begin. . . .

VOICES. Herod for ever.

PILATE.   Let us go within. . . .

HEROD. Yes. By the by, what happened to
the man?

I sent him back to you; a rumor ran

That he was crucified.

PILATE.   He was.

HEROD.   The priests

Rage upon points of doctrine at the feasts.

VOICES. God bless you, Herod; give you
length of days, Herod.

HEROD [*to the* CROWD]. Go home. To God
alone give praise.

This is Deliverance Night; go home, for soon

Over the dusty hill will come the moon,

And you must feast, with prayer to the Adored.

[*To* PILATE.] He well deserved his death.

VOICES.   God bless you, Lord.

PILATE. I'll lead the way. . . .

VOICES.   Herod.

HEROD [*to* PROCULA].   Lady, your hand.

PROCULA. There is a just man's blood upon
    the sand.

Mind how you tread.

> *They go in.   The bronze doors are*
> *closed.   The* CROWD *remains for an in-*
> *stant watching the doors.*

A VOICE. Herod the Fox makes friends with
    Pilate.   Why?

A VOICE. He needs a Roman loan.

A VOICE.   Look at the sky,
The Paschal moon has risen.

A VOICE.   God is great.
Why did I linger here?   I shall be late. [*Going.*]

A VOICE. Good night and blessing.

A VOICE [*going*].   Pilate's color changed
When we cheered Herod.

A VOICE.   They have been estranged

A long while now; but now they will be friends.
    [*Going.*]

  A Voice. What joy it is when Preparation
    ends.

Now to our Feast.   Do you go down the stair?

  A Voice. Yes, past the pools; will you come
    with me there?

  A Voice. I love to walk by moonlight; let
    us go.   [*They go.*]

  A Voice [*singing*]. Friends, out of Egypt,
    long ago,

Our wandering fathers came,

Treading the paths that God did show

By pointing cloud and flame.

By land and sea His darkness and His light

Led us into His peace. . . .   [*The voice dies
    away.*]

  A Voice [*off*].   Good-night.

    Only The Madman *remains.   He takes
    lilies from a box and begins to tie them in
    bunches.*

MADMAN. Only a penny, a penny,

Lilies brighter than any,

Lilies whiter than snow.　[*He feels that he is
　　alone.*]

Beautiful lilies grow

Wherever the truth so sweet

Has trodden with bloody feet,

Has stood with a bloody brow.

Friend, it is over now,

The passion, the sweat, the pains,

Only the truth remains.　[*He lays lilies down.*]

*　　*　　*　　*　　*　　*

I cannot see what others see;

Wisdom alone is kind to me,

Wisdom that comes from Agony.

*　　*　　*　　*　　*　　*

Wisdom that lives in the pure skies,

The untouched star, the spirit's eyes;

O Beauty, touch me, make me wise.

CURTAIN.

SONNETS

NOTE

Some few of these sonnets appeared serially in the *Atlantic Monthly*, *Scribner's Magazine*, *Harper's Monthly*, and (perhaps) in one or two other papers. I thank the Editors of these papers for permission to reprint them here.

JOHN MASEFIELD.

LONDON, 16th Dec. 1915.

Long long ago, when all the glittering earth
Was heaven itself, when drunkards in the street
Were like mazed kings shaking at giving birth
To acts of war that sickle men like wheat,
When the white clover opened Paradise
And God lived in a cottage up the brook,
Beauty, you lifted up my sleeping eyes
And filled my heart with longing with a look;
And all the day I searched but could not find
The beautiful dark-eyed who touched me there,
Delight in her made trouble in my mind,
She was within all Nature, everywhere,
The breath I breathed, the brook, the flower,
      the grass,
Were her, her word, her beauty, all she was.

Night came again, but now I could not sleep.

The owls were watching in the yew, the mice

Gnawed at the wainscot; the mid dark was
      deep,

The death-watch knocked the dead man's
      summons thrice.

The cats upon the pointed housetops peered

About the chimneys, with lit eyes which saw

Things in the darkness, moving, which they
      feared.

The midnight filled the quiet house with awe.

So, creeping down the stair, I drew the bolt

And passed into the darkness, and I knew

That Beauty was brought near by my revolt.

Beauty was in the moonlight, in the dew,

But more within myself whose venturous tread

Walked the dark house where death ticks called
      the dead.

Even after all these years there comes the dream
Of lovelier life than this in some new earth,
In the full summer of that unearthly gleam
Which lights the spirit when the brain gives
      birth,
Of a perfected I, in happy hours,
Treading above the sea that trembles there,
A path through thickets of immortal flowers
That only grow where sorrows never were.
And, at a turn, of coming face to face
With Beauty's self, that Beauty I have sought
In women's hearts, in friends, in many a place,
In barren hours passed at grips with thought,
Beauty of woman, comrade, earth and sea,
Incarnate thought come face to face with me.

If I could come again to that dear place
Where once I came, where Beauty lived and
       moved,
Where, by the sea, I saw her face to face,
That soul alive by which the world has loved;
If, as I stood at gaze among the leaves,
She would appear again, as once before,
While the red herdsman gathered up his sheaves
And brimming waters trembled up the shore;
If, as I gazed, her Beauty that was dumb,
In that old time, before I learned to speak,
Would lean to me and revelation come,
Words to the lips and color to the cheek,
Joy with its searing-iron would burn me wise,
I should know all; all powers, all mysteries.

Men are made human by the mighty fall
The mighty passion led to, these remain.
The despot, at the last assaulted wall,
By long disaster is made man again,
The faithful fool who follows the torn flag,
The woman marching by the beaten man,
Make with their truth atonement for the brag,
And earn a pity for the too proud plan.
For in disaster, in the ruined will,
In the soiled shreds of what the brain conceived,
Something above the wreck is steady still,
Bright above all that cannot be retrieved,
Grandeur of soul, a touching of the star
That good days cover but by which we are.

Here in the self is all that man can know
Of Beauty, all the wonder, all the power,
All the unearthly color, all the glow,
Here in the self which withers like a flower;
Here in the self which fades as hours pass,
And droops and dies and rots and is forgotten,
Sooner, by ages, than the mirroring glass
In which it sees its glory still unrotten.
Here in the flesh, within the flesh, behind,
Swift in the blood and throbbing on the bone,
Beauty herself, the universal mind,
Eternal April wandering alone,
The god, the holy ghost, the atoning lord,
Here in the flesh, the never yet explored.

Flesh, I have knocked at many a dusty door,
Gone down full many a windy midnight lane,
Probed in old walls and felt along the floor,
Pressed in blind hope the lighted window-pane.
But useless all, though sometimes, when the
      moon
Was full in heaven and the sea was full,
Along my body's alleys came a tune
Played in the tavern by the Beautiful.
Then for an instant I have felt at point
To find and seize her, whosoe'er she be,
Whether some saint whose glory does anoint
Those whom she loves, or but a part of me,
Or something that the things not understood
Make for their uses out of flesh and blood.

But all has passed, the tune has died away,
The glamour gone, the glory; is it chance?
Is the unfeeling mud stabbed by a ray
Cast by an unseen splendor's great advance?
Or does the glory gather crumb by crumb
Unseen, within, as coral islands rise,
Till suddenly the apparitions come
Above the surface, looking at the skies?
Or does sweet Beauty dwell in lovely things,
Scattering the holy hintings of her name
In women, in dear friends, in flowers, in springs,
In the brook's voice, for us to catch the same?
Or is it we who are Beauty, we who ask,
We by whose gleams the world fulfils its task?

These myriad days, these many thousand hours,
A man's long life, so choked with dusty things,
How little perfect poise with perfect powers,
Joy at the heart and Beauty at the springs.
One hour, or two, or three, in long years scat-
       tered,
Sparks from a smithy that have fired a thatch,
Are all that life has given and all that mattered,
The rest, all heaving at a moveless latch.
For these, so many years of useless toil,
Despair, endeavor, and again despair,
Sweat, that the base machine may have its oil,
Idle delight to tempt one everywhere.
A life upon the cross.   To make amends
Three flaming memories that the deathbed ends.

There, on the darkened deathbed, dies the
      brain
That flared three several times in seventy years;
It cannot lift the silly hand again,
Nor speak, nor sing, it neither sees nor hears.
And muffled mourners put it in the ground
And then go home, and in the earth it lies,
Too dark for vision and too deep for sound,
The million cells that made a good man wise.
Yet for a few short years an influence stirs
A sense or wraith or essence of him dead,
Which makes insensate things its ministers
To those beloved, his spirit's daily bread;
Then that, too, fades; in book or deed a spark
Lingers, then that, too, fades; then all is dark.

So in the empty sky the stars appear,
Are bright in heaven marching through the sky,
Spinning their planets, each one to his year,
Tossing their fiery hair until they die;
Then in the tower afar the watcher sees
The sun, that burned, less noble than it was,
Less noble still, until by dim degrees,
No spark of him is specklike in his glass.
Then blind and dark in heaven the sun proceeds,
Vast, dead and hideous, knocking on his moons,
Till crashing on his like creation breeds,
Striking such life a constellation swoons.
From dead things striking fire a new sun springs,
New fire, new life, new planets with new wings.

It may be so with us, that in the dark,
When we have done with Time and wander
    Space,
Some meeting of the blind may strike a spark,
And to Death's empty mansion give a grace.
It may be, that the loosened soul may find
Some new delight of living without limbs,
Bodiless joy of flesh-untrammelled mind,
Peace like a sky where starlike spirit swims.
It may be, that the million cells of sense,
Loosed from their seventy years' adhesion, pass
Each to some joy of changed experience,
Weight in the earth or glory in the grass;
It may be that we cease; we cannot tell.
Even if we cease life is a miracle.

Man has his unseen friend, his unseen twin,
His straitened spirit's possibility,
The palace unexplored he thinks an inn,
The glorious garden which he wanders by.
It is beside us while we clutch at clay
To daub ourselves that we may never see.
Like the lame donkey lured by moving hay
We chase the shade but let the real be.
Yet, when confusion in our heaven brings stress,
We thrust on that unseen, get stature from it,
Cast to the devil's challenge the man's yes,
And stream our fiery hour like a comet,
And know for that fierce hour a friend behind,
With sword and shield, the second to the mind.

What am I, Life?   A thing of watery salt
Held in cohesion by unresting cells,
Which work they know not why, which never
          halt,
Myself unwitting where their Master dwells.
I do not bid them, yet they toil, they spin;
A world which uses me as I use them,
Nor do I know which end or which begin
Nor which to praise, which pamper, which con-
          demn.
So, like a marvel in a marvel set,
I answer to the vast, as wave by wave
The sea of air goes over, dry or wet,
Or the full moon comes swimming from her
          cave,
Or the great sun comes north, this myriad I
Tingles, not knowing how, yet wondering why.

If I could get within this changing I,
This ever altering thing which yet persists,
Keeping the features it is reckoned by,
While each component atom breaks or twists,
If, wandering past strange groups of shifting
     forms,
Cells at their hidden marvels hard at work,
Pale from much toil, or red from sudden storms,
I might attain to where the Rulers lurk.
If, pressing past the guards in those grey gates,
The brain's most folded intertwisted shell,
I might attain to that which alters fates,
The King, the supreme self, the Master Cell,
Then, on Man's earthly peak, I might behold
The unearthly self beyond, unguessed, untold.

What is this atom which contains the whole,
This miracle which needs adjuncts so strange,
This, which imagined God and is the soul,
The steady star persisting amid change?
What waste, that smallness of such power
     should need
Such clumsy tools so easy to destroy,
Such wasteful servants difficult to feed,
Such indirect dark avenues to joy.
Why, if its business is not mainly earth,
Should it demand such heavy chains to sense?
A heavenly thing demands a swifter birth,
A quicker hand to act intelligence.
An earthly thing were better like the rose
At peace with clay from which its beauty
     grows.

Ah, we are neither heaven nor earth, but men;
Something that uses and despises both,
That takes its earth's contentment in the pen,
Then sees the world's injustice and is wroth,
And flinging off youth's happy promise, flies
Up to some breach, despising earthly things,
And, in contempt of hell and heaven, dies,
Rather than bear some yoke of priests or kings.
Our joys are not of heaven nor earth, but man's,
A woman's beauty or a child's delight,
The trembling blood when the discoverer scans
The sought-for world, the guessed-at satellite;
The ringing scene, the stone at point to blush
For unborn men to look at and say "Hush."

Roses are beauty, but I never see
Those blood drops from the burning heart of
      June
Glowing like thought upon the living tree,
Without a pity that they die so soon,
Die into petals, like those roses old,
Those women, who were summer in men's
      hearts
Before the smile upon the Sphinx was cold,
Or sand had hid the Syrian and his arts.
O myriad dust of beauty that lies thick
Under our feet that not a single grain
But stirred and moved in beauty and was quick
For one brief moon and died nor lived again;
But when the moon rose lay upon the grass
Pasture to living beauty, life that was.

Over the church's door they moved a stone
And there, unguessed, forgotten, mortared up,
Lay the priest's cell where he had lived alone;
There was his ashy hearth, his drinking cup;
There was the window whence he saw the host,
The god whose beauty quickened bread and
       wine,
The skeleton of a religion lost,
The ghostless bones of what had been divine.
O many a time the dusty masons come,
Knocking their trowels in the stony brain,
To cells where perished priests had once a home,
Or where devout brows pressed the window pane,
Watching the thing made God, the god whose
       bones
Bind underground our soul's foundation stones.

I never see the red rose crown the year,
Nor feel the young grass underneath my tread,
Without the thought "This living beauty here
Is earth's remembrance of a beauty dead.
Surely where all this glory is displayed
Love has been quick, like fire, to high ends,
Here, in this grass, an altar has been made
For some white joy, some sacrifice of friends;
Here, where I stand, some leap of human
            brains
Has touched immortal things and left its trace,
The earth is happy here, the gleam remains;
Beauty is here, the spirit of the place,
I touch the faith which nothing can destroy,
The earth, the living church of ancient joy."

Out of the clouds come torrents, from the earth
Fire and quakings, from the shrieking air
Tempests that harry half the planet's girth.
Death's unseen seeds are scattered every-
      where.
Yet in his iron cage the mind of man
Measures and braves the terrors of all these,
The blindest fury and the subtlest plan
He turns, or tames, or shows in their degrees.
Yet in himself are forces of like power,
Untamed, unreckoned; seeds that brain to brain
Pass across oceans bringing thought to flower,
New worlds, new selves, where he can live again,
Eternal beauty's everlasting rose
Which casts this world as shadow as it goes.

O little self, within whose smallness lies
All that man was, and is, and will become,
Atom unseen that comprehends the skies
And tells the tracks by which the planets roam.
That, without moving, knows the joys of
        wings,
The tiger's strength, the eagle's secrecy,
And in the hovel can consort with kings,
Or clothe a god with his own mystery.
O with what darkness do we cloak thy light,
What dusty folly gather thee for food,
Thou who alone art knowledge and delight,
The heavenly bread, the beautiful, the good.
O living self, O god, O morning star,
Give us thy light, forgive us what we are.

I went into the fields, but you were there
Waiting for me, so all the summer flowers
Were only glimpses of your starry powers,
Beautiful and inspired dust they were.
I went down by the waters, and a bird
Sang with your voice in all the unknown tones
Of all that self of you I have not heard,
So that my being felt you to the bones.
I went into my house, and shut the door
To be alone, but you were there with me;
All beauty in a little room may be
Though the roof lean and muddy be the floor.
Then in my bed I bound my tired eyes
To make a darkness for my weary brain,
But like a presence you were there again,
Being and real, beautiful and wise,
So that I could not sleep and cried aloud,
"You strange grave thing, what is it you would
          say?"
The redness of your dear lips dimmed to grey,
The waters ebbed, the moon hid in a cloud.

There are two forms of life, of which one moves,
Seeking its meat in many forms of Death,
On scales, on wings, on all the myriad hooves
Which stamp earth's exultation in quick breath.
It rustles through the reeds in shivering fowl,
Cries over moors in curlew, glitters green
In the lynx' eye, is fearful in the howl
Of winter-bitten wolves whose flanks are lean.
It takes dumb joy in cattle, it is fierce,
It torts the tiger's loin, the eagle's wings,
Its tools are claws to smite and teeth to pierce,
Arms to destroy, and coils, and poison stings;
Wherever earth is quick and life runs red
Its mark is death, its meat is something dead.

Restless and hungry, still it moves and slays

Feeding its beauty on dead beauty's bones,

Most merciless in all its million ways,

Its breath for singing bought by dying groans,

Roving so far with such a zest to kill

(Its strongness adding hunger) that at last

Its cells attain beyond the cruel skill

To where life's earliest impulses are past.

Then this creation of the linkéd lusts,

To move and eat, still under their control,

Hunts for his prey in thought, his thinking
      thrusts

Through the untrodden jungle of the soul,

Through slip and quag, morasses dripping
      green,

Seeking the thing supposed but never seen.

How many ways, how many different times
The tiger Mind has clutched at what it sought,
Only to prove supposéd virtues crimes,
The imagined godhead but a form of thought.
How many restless brains have wrought and
     schemed,
Padding their cage, or built, or brought to law,
Made in outlasting brass the something dreamed,
Only to prove themselves the things of awe,
Yet, in the happy moment's lightning blink,
Comes scent, or track, or trace, the game goes
     by,
Some leopard thought is pawing at the brink,
Chaos below, and, up above, the sky.
Then the keen nostrils scent, about, about,
To prove the Thing Within a Thing Without.

The other form of Living does not stir;
Where the seed chances there it roots and grows,
To suck what makes the lily or the fir
Out of the earth and from the air that blows.

Great power of Will that little thing the seed
Has, all alone in earth, to plan the tree,
And, though the mud oppresses, to succeed,
And put out branches where the birds may be.

Then the wind blows it, but the bending boughs
Exult like billows, and their million green
Drink the all-living sunlight in carouse,
Like dainty harts where forest wells are clean.

While it, the central plant, which looks o'er
    miles,
Draws milk from the earth's breast, and sways,
    and smiles.

Is there a great green commonwealth of Thought
Which ranks the yearly pageant, and decides
How Summer's royal progress shall be wrought,
By secret stir which in each plant abides?
Does rocking daffodil consent that she,
The snowdrop of wet winters, shall be first?
Does spotted cowslip with the grass agree
To hold her pride before the rattle burst?
And in the hedge what quick agreement goes,
When hawthorn blossoms redden to decay,
That Summer's pride shall come, the Summer's
      rose,
Before the flower be on the bramble spray?
Or is it, as with us, unresting strife,
And each consent a lucky gasp for life?

Beauty, let be; I cannot see your face,
I shall not know you now, nor touch your feet,
Only within me tremble to your grace
Tasting this crumb vouchsafed which is so
    sweet.
Even when the full-leaved Summer bore no
    fruit,
You give me this, this apple of man's tree;
This planet sings when other spheres were mute,
This light begins when darkness covered me.
Now, though I know that I shall never know
All, through my fault, nor blazon with my pen
That path prepared where only I could go,
Still, I have this, not given to other men.
Beauty, this grace, this spring, this given
    bread,
This life, this dawn, this wakening from the
    dead.

Here, where we stood together, we three men,
Before the war had swept us to the East
Three thousand miles away, I stand again
And hear the bells, and breathe, and go to feast.
We trod the same path, to the self-same place,
Yet here I stand, having beheld their graves,
Skyros whose shadows the great seas erase,
And Seddul Bahr that ever more blood craves.
So, since we communed here, our bones have
        been
Nearer, perhaps, than they again will be,
Earth and the world-wide battle lie between,
Death lies between, and friend-destroying sea.
Yet here, a year ago, we talked and stood
As I stand now, with pulses beating blood.

I saw her like a shadow on the sky
In the last light, a blur upon the sea,
Then the gale's darkness put the shadow by,
But from one grave that island talked to me;
And, in the midnight, in the breaking storm,
I saw its blackness and a blinking light,
And thought, "So death obscures your gentle
      form,
So memory strives to make the darkness bright;
And, in that heap of rocks, your body lies,
Part of the island till the planet ends,
My gentle comrade, beautiful and wise,
Part of this crag this bitter surge offends,
While I, who pass, a little obscure thing,
War with this force, and breathe, and am its
      king."

Not that the stars are all gone mad in heaven
Plucking the unseen reins upon men's souls,
Not that the law that bound the planets seven
Is discord now; man probes for new controls.
He bends no longer to the circling stars,
New moon and full moon and the living sun,
Love-making Venus, Jove and bloody Mars
Pass from their thrones, their rule of him is
          done.
And paler gods, made liker men, are past,
Like their sick eras to their funeral urns,
They cannot stand the fire blown by the blast
In which man's soul that measures heaven burns.
Man in his cage of many millioned pain
Burns all to ash to prove if God remain.

There is no God, as I was taught in youth,
Though each, according to his stature, builds
Some covered shrine for what he thinks the
      truth,
Which day by day his reddest heart-blood gilds.
There is no God; but death, the clasping sea,
In which we move like fish, deep over deep
Made of men's souls that bodies have set free,
Floods to a Justice though it seems asleep.
There is no God, but still, behind the veil,
The hurt thing works, out of its agony.
Still, like a touching of a brimming Grail,
Return the pennies given to passers by.
There is no God, but we, who breathe the air,
Are God ourselves and touch God everywhere.

Beauty retires; the blood out of the earth
Shrinks, the stalk dries, lifeless November still
Drops the brown husk of April's greenest birth.
Through the thinned beech clump I can see
    the hill.
So withers man, and though his life renews
In Aprils of the soul, an autumn comes
Which gives an end, not respite, to the thews
That bore his soul through the world's martyr-
    doms.
Then all the beauty will be out of mind,
Part of man's store, that lies outside his brain,
Touch to the dead and vision to the blind,
Drink in the desert, bread, eternal grain;
Part of the untilled field that beauty sows
With flowers untold, where quickened spirit
    goes.

Wherever beauty has been quick in clay
Some effluence of it lives, a spirit dwells,
Beauty that death can never take away,
Mixed with the air that shakes the flower bells;
So that by waters where the apples fall,
Or in lone glens, or valleys full of flowers,
Or in the streets where bloody tidings call,
The haunting waits the mood that makes it
       ours.
Then at a turn, a word, an act, a thought,
Such difference comes, the spirit apprehends
That place's glory, for where beauty fought
Under the veil the glory never ends,
But the still grass, the leaves, the trembling
       flower,
Keep, through dead time, that everlasting hour.

You are more beautiful than women are,
Wiser than men, stronger than ribbéd death,
Juster than Time, more constant than the star,
Dearer than love, more intimate than breath;
Having all art, all science, all control
Over the still unsmithied, even as Time
Cradles the generations of man's soul,
You are the light to guide, the way to climb.
So, having followed beauty, having bowed
To wisdom and to death, to law, to power,
I like a blind man stumble from the crowd
Into the darkness of a deeper hour,
Where in the lonely silence I may wait
The prayed-for gleam—your hand upon the
gate.

Out of the barracks to the castle yard

Those Roman soldiers came, buckling their gear;

The word was passed that they were prison
guard;

The sergeant proved their dressing with his
spear.

Then, as the prisoner came, a wretch who bled

Holding a cross, those nearest cursed his soul:

He might have died some other time, they said,

Not at high noon: the sergeant called the roll.

Then, sloping spears, the files passed from the
court

Into the alleys, thrusting back the crowd,

They cursed the bleeding man for stepping
short;

The drums beat time: the sergeant hummed
aloud;

The rabble closed behind: the soldiers cursed

The prisoner's soul, the flies, their packs, their
thirst.

Not for the anguish suffered is the slur,
Not for the women's mocks, the taunts of men,
No, but because you never welcomed her,
Her of whose beauty I am only the pen.
There was a dog, dog-minded, with dog's eyes,
Damned by a dog's brute-nature to be true,
Something within her made his spirit wise,
He licked her hand, he knew her, not so you.
When all adulterate beauty has gone by,
When all inanimate matter has gone down,
We will arise and walk, that dog and I,
The only two who knew her in the town,
We'll range the pleasant mountains side by
    side,
Seeking the blood-stained flowers where Christs
    have died.

Beauty was with me once, but now, grown old,

I cannot hear nor see her: thus a king

In the high turret kept him from the cold

Over the fire, with his magic ring

Which, as he wrought, made pictures come and
go

Of men and times, past, present, and to be,

Now like a smoke, now flame-like, now a glow,

Now dead, now bright, but always fantasy.

While, on the stair without, a faithful slave

Stabbed to the death, crawled bleeding, whisper-
ing "Sir,

They come to kill you, fly: I come to save;

O you great gods, have pity, let him hear."

Then, with his last strength tapped and mut-
tered, "Sire,"

While the king smiled and drowsed above the
fire.

So beauty comes, so with a failing hand
She knocks and cries, and fails to make me hear,
She who tells futures in the falling sand
And still, by signs, makes hidden meanings clear;
She, who behind this many peopled smoke,
Moves in the light and struggles to direct,
Through the deaf ear and by the baffled stroke,
The wicked man, the honored architect.
Yet at a dawn before the birds begin,
In dreams, as the horse stamps and the hound
        stirs,
Sleep slips the bolt and beauty enters in
Crying aloud those hurried words of hers,
And I awake and, in the birded dawn,
Know her for Queen and own myself a pawn.

If Beauty be at all, if, beyond sense,
There be a wisdom piercing into brains,
Why should the glory wait on impotence,
Biding its time till blood is in the veins?
There is no beauty, but, when thought is quick,
Out of the noisy sickroom of ourselves,
Some flattery comes to try to cheat the sick,
Some drowsy drug is groped for on the shelves.
And, for the rest, we play upon a scene
Beautiful with the blood of living things;
We move and speak and wonder and have been,
Upon the dust as dust, not queens and kings;
We know no beauty, nor does beauty care
For us, this dust, that men make everywhere.

Each greedy self, by consecrating lust,
Desire pricking into sacrifice,
Adds, in his way, some glory to the dust,
Brings, to the light, some haze of Paradise,
Hungers and thirsts for beauty; like the hound
Snaps it, to eat alone; in secret keeps
His miser's patch of consecrated ground
Where beauty's coins are dug down to the deeps.
So when disturbing death digs up our lives,
Some little gleam among the broken soil
May witness for us as the shovel rives
The dirty heap of all our tiny toil;
Some gleam of you may make the digger hold,
Touched for an instant with the thought of
     gold.

Time being an instant in eternity,
Beauty above man's million years must see
The heaped corrupted mass that had to die,
The husk of man that set the glitter free;
Now from those million bodies in the dark,
Forgotten, rotten, part of fields or roads,
The million gleam united makes a spark
Which Beauty sees among her star abodes.
And, from the bodies, comes a sigh, "Alas,
We hated, fought and killed, as separate men;
Now all is merged and we are in the grass,
Our efforts merged, would we had known it then.
All our lives' battle, all our spirits' dream,
Nought in themselves, a clash which made a
      gleam."

You will remember me in days to come
With love, or pride, or pity, or contempt;
So will my friends (not many friends, yet some)
When this my life will be a dream out-dreamt;
And one, remembering friendship by the fire,
And one, remembering love time in the dark,
And one, remembering unfulfilled desire,
Will sigh, perhaps, yet be beside the mark;
For this my body with its wandering ghost
Is nothing solely but an empty grange,
Dark in a night that owls inhabit most,
Yet when the king rides by there comes a change;
The windows gleam, the cresset's fiery hair
Blasts the blown branch and beauty lodges
     there.

They took the bloody body from the cross,
They laid it in its niche and rolled the stone.
One said, "Our blessed Master," one "His loss
Ends us companions, we are left alone."
And one, "I thought that Pilate would acquit
Right to the last;" and one, "The sergeant took
The trenching mall and drove the nails with it."
One who was weeping went apart and shook.
Then one, "He promised that in three short
     days
He would return, oh God; but He is dead."
And one, "What was it that He meant to raise?
The Temple? No? What was it that He said?
He said that He would build? That He would
     rise?"
"No," answered one, "but come from Paradise.

"Come to us fiery with the saints of God

To judge the world and take His power and
reign."

Then one. "This was the very road we trod

That April day, would it could come again;

The day they flung the flowers." "Let be,"
said one,

"He was a lovely soul, but what He meant

Passes our wit, for none among us, none,

Had brains enough to fathom His intent.

His mother did not, nor could one of us,

But while He spoke I felt I understood."

And one, "He knew that it would finish thus.

Let His thought be, I know that He was good.

There is the orchard see, the very same

Where we were sleeping when the soldiers
came."

So from the cruel cross they buried God;

So, in their desolation, as they went

They dug him deeper with each step they trod,

Their lightless minds distorting what He meant.

Lamenting Him, their leader, who had died,

They heaped the stones, they rolled the heavy
     door;

They said, "Our glory has been crucified,

Unless He rise our glory will be o'er."

While in the grave the spirit left the corpse

Broken by torture, slowly, line by line,

And saw the dawn come on the eastern thorpes,

And shook his wings and sang in the divine,

Crying "I told the truth, even unto death,

Though I was earth and now am only breath."

If all be governed by the moving stars,
If passing planets bring events to be,
Searing the face of Time with bloody scars,
Drawing men's souls even as the moon the sea;
If as they pass they make a current pass
Across man's life and heap it to a tide,
We are but pawns, ignobler than the grass
Cropped by the beast and crunched and tossed
      aside.
Is all this beauty that does inhabit heaven
Trail of a planet's fire?   Is all this lust
A chymic means by warring stars contriven
To bring the violets out of Cæsar's dust?
Better be grass, or in some hedge unknown
The spilling rose whose beauty is its own.

In emptiest furthest heaven where no stars are
Perhaps some planet of our master sun
Still rolls an unguessed orbit round its star
Unthought, unseen, unknown of any one.
Roving dead space according to its law
Casting our light on burnt-out suns and blind
Singing in the frozen void its word of awe
One wandering thought in all that idiot mind.
And, in some span of many a thousand year,
Passing through heaven, its influence may arouse
Beauty unguessed in those who habit here,
And men may rise with glory on their brows,
And feel new life like fire, and see the old
Fall from them dead, the bronze's broken mould.

Perhaps in chasms of the wasted past,
That planet wandered within hail of ours,
And plucked men's souls to loveliness and cast
The old, that was, away, like husks of flowers;
And made them stand erect and bade them build
Nobler than hovels plaited in the mire,
Gave them an altar and a god to gild,
Bridled the brooks for them and fettered fire;
And, in another coming, forged the steel
Which, on life's scarlet wax, forever set
Longing for beauty bitten as a seal
That blood not clogs nor centuries forget,
That built Atlantis, and, in time will raise
That grander thing whose image haunts our
         days.

For, like an outcast from the city, I
Wander the desert strewn with traveller's bones,
Having no comrade but the starry sky
Where the tuned planets ride their floating
    thrones.
I pass old ruins where the kings caroused
In cups long shards from vines long since de-
    cayed,
I tread the broken brick where queens were
    housed
In beauty's time ere beauty was betrayed;
And in the ceaseless pitting of the sand
On monolith and pyle, I see the dawn,
Making those skeletons of beauty grand
By fire that comes as darkness is withdrawn;
And in that fire the art of men to come
Shines with such glow I bless my martyrdom.

Death lies in wait for you, you wild thing in the
      wood,
Shy-footed beauty dear, half-seen, half-under-
      stood,
Glimpsed in the beech wood dim, and in the
      dropping fir,
Shy like a fawn and sweet and beauty's minister.
Glimpsed as in flying clouds by night the little
      moon,
A wonder, a delight, a paleness passing soon.

Only a moment held, only an hour seen,
Only an instant known in all that life has been,
One instant in the sand to drink that gush of grace
The beauty of your way, the marvel of your face.

Death lies in wait for you, but few short hours
      he gives,
I perish even as you by whom all spirit lives,
Come to me, spirit, come, and fill my hour of
      breath
With hours of life in life that pay no toll to death.

What are we given, what do we take away?
Five little senses, startling with delight,
That dull to death and perish into clay
And pass from human memory as from sight.
So the new penny glittering from the mint,
Bears the king's head awhile, but Time effaces
The head, the date, the seated queen, the print
Even as a brook the stone in pebbly places.
We bear the stamp, are current, and are prized,
Hoarded or spent, the while the mintage passes,
Then, like light money, challenged or despised,
We join the heap of dross which Time amasses,
Erased, uncurrent discs no more to range
The clanging counters in the great exchange.

They called that broken hedge The Haunted
    Gate.
Strange fires (they said) burnt there at moonless
    times.
Evil was there, men never went there late,
The darkness there was quick with threatened
    crimes.
And then one digging in that bloodied clay
Found, but a foot below, a rotted chest.
Coins of the Romans, tray on rusted tray,
Hurriedly heaped there by a digger prest.
So that one knew how, centuries before,
Some Roman flying from the sack by night,
Digging in terror there to hide his store,
Sweating his pick, by windy lantern light,
Had stamped his anguish on that place's soul,
So that it knew and could rehearse the whole.

There was an evil in the nodding wood
Above the quarry long since overgrown,
Something which stamped it as a place of blood
Where tortured spirit cried from murdered
     bone.
Then, after years, I saw a rusty knife
Stuck in a woman's skull, just as 'twas found,
Blackt with a centuried crust of clotted life,
In the red clay of that unholy ground.
So that I knew the unhappy thing had spoken,
That tongueless thing for whom the quarry
     spoke,
The evil seals of murder had been broken
By the red earth, the grass, the rooted oak,
The inarticulate dead had forced the spade,
The hand, the mind, till murder was displayed.

Go, spend your penny, Beauty, when you will,

In the grave's darkness let the stamp be lost.

The water still will bubble from the hill,

And April quick the meadows with her ghost;

Over the grass the daffodils will shiver,

The primroses with their pale beauty abound,

The blackbird be a lover and make quiver

With his glad singing the great soul of the
    ground;

So that if the body rot, it will not matter;

Up in the earth the great game will go on,

The coming of Spring and the running of the
    water,

And the young things glad of the womb's
    darkness gone;

And the joy we felt will be a part of the glory

In the lover's kiss that makes the old couple's
    story.

Not for your human beauty nor the power
To shake me by your voice or by your touch,
Summer must have its rose, the rose must
      flower,
Beauty burn deep, I do not yield to such.
No, but because your beauty where it falls
Lays bare the spirits in the crowded streets,
Shatters the lock, destroys the castle walls,
Breaks down the bars till friend with comrade
      meets,
So that I wander brains where beauty dwelled
In long dead time, and see again the rose
By long dead men for living beauty held,
That Death's knife spares, and Winter with his
      snows,
And know it bloodied by that pulse of birth
Which greens the grass in Aprils upon earth.

The little robin hopping in the wood
Draws friendship from you, the rapt nightingale
Making the night a marvellous solitude,
Only of you to darkness tells the tale.
Kingfishers are but jewels on your dress,
Dun deer that rove and timid rabbits shy
Are but the hintings of your gentleness.
Upon your wings the eagle climbs the sky.
Fish that are shadows in the water pass
With mystery from you, the purpled moth
Dust from your kirtle on his broidery has,
Out of your bounty every beauty flowth.
For you are all, all fire, all living form,
Marvel in man and glory in the worm.

Though in life's streets the tempting shops have
      lured,

Because all beauty, howsoever base,

Is vision of you, marred, I have endured

Tempted or fall'n, to look upon your face.

Now through the grinning death's head in the
      paint,

Within the tavern-song, hid in the wine,

In many kinded man, emperor and saint,

I see you pass, you breath of the divine.

I see you pass, as centuries ago

The long dead men with passionate spirit saw,

O brother man, whom spirit habits so,

Through your red sorrows Beauty keeps her
      law,

Beauty herself, who takes your dying hand,

To leave through Time the Memnon in the sand.

When all these million cells that are my slaves
Fall from my pourried ribs and leave me lone,
A living speck among a world of graves,
What shall I be, that spot in the unknown?
A glow-worm in a night that floats the sun?
Or deathless dust feeling the passer's foot?
An eye undying mourning things undone?
Or seed for quickening free from prisoning
　　　fruit?
Or an eternal jewel on your robe,
Caught to your heart, one with the April fire
That made me yours as man upon the globe,
One with the Spring, a breath in all desire,
One with the primrose, present in all joy?
Or pash that rots, which pismires can destroy?

Let that which is to come be as it may,

Darkness, extinction, justice, life intense,

The flies are happy in the summer day,

Flies will be happy many summers hence.

Time with his antique breeds that built the
       Sphynx

Time with her men to come whose wings will
       tower,

Poured and will pour, not as the wise man
       thinks,

But with blind force, to each his little hour.

And when the hour has struck, comes death or
       change,

Which, whether good or ill, we cannot tell,

But the blind planet will wander through her
       range

Bearing men like us who will serve as well.

The sun will rise, the winds that ever move

Will blow our dust that once were men in love.

THE MADMAN'S SONG

You have not seen what I have seen,
The town besieged by a million men;
I saw it though, the people starved,
My rib-bones here came through my skin.

Thousands were killed and thousands died,
We ate dead blow-flies from the stalls;
"Help us, O Lord, our King," we cried;
He could not help, for all our calls.

No, but there was a poor mean man,
A skinny man and mad, like me,
He saw: he told the King his plan,
A plan to set our city free.

The King in fury had him bound,
Dragged to the walls with kick and curse,
And flung from off them to the ground;
Daily our agonies grew worse.

And all our sallies came to wreck,
We ate the dead men from the grave,

Our troops were killed or put in check,
"O King," we cried, "in pity, save,
Save us or we shall die," we cried.
He could not save us, so we died.

        *   *   *   *   *   *

But then he called to mind the man
Whose bones the dogs had picked by this,
He murmured, "We will try the plan,
Death would be better than what is.
I'll try the madman's plan to-night.
Do I remember it aright?"

        *   *   *   *   *   *

We did the madman's will, we won,
We left the million rotting there;
Not one remained alive, not one,
The madman's wisdom was most rare.
We laughed, we ate again, we drank,
Rebuilt the city, walls and towers,
We cried "We have the King to thank."
We strewed his royal path with flowers.

        *   *   *   *   *   *

But I who am mad am wiser now,

I wander in the city ditch,

For wisdom grows on the withered bough.

Flowers are fair and fruit is rich,

But wisdom is lovelier than them all.

So when the world is hard at work,

I kneel in the foss below the wall

On the rubble where the lizards lurk.

*   *   *   *   *   *

The goutweed hides the poor man's bones,

The mint-scent warms in the hot air,

An influence comes out of the stones,

The dead man's spirit quickens there,

Singing, "I trod the piteous way

The world despised me, comrades failed,

But from above an unquenched ray

Burned in my brain: it never quailed;

My body shook, my mind had doubt,

That star within me helped me on,

Man, the walled town which cast me out,

Was powerless like a fever gone.

And now I know that light is like the sea,

I was the rock it girt, it beat on me.

I was the deaf-mute, blinded by a curse,

Outside me was the starry universe

I had but to unlatch to let it in.

Nothing but mental blindness can be sin,

All seeing saves, all hearing, all delight,

I am a star. I wander through the night."

Printed in the United States of America.

THE following pages contain advertisements of Macmillan books by the same author.

John M. Synge: A Few Personal Recollections

Boards, 8vo, $1.50.

"The kind of description that would have pleased Synge—being quite free from sentiment or any kind of heroics."—*The Independent.*

Philip the King and Other Poems

Cloth, 12mo, $1.25; leather, $1.50.

"Cannot fail to increase the already great reputation of John Masefield as a poetic dramatist. . . . Full of poetic imagination and dramatic force."— *The Nation.*

The Tragedy of Pompey the Great

Cloth, 12mo, $1.25; leather, $1.50.

"He is no statuesque Pompey, spouting prose lines masquerading as poetry. Masefield has given us Pompey the man. He has made human the men who surrounded the old Roman. And his drama is in modern prose, yet strikes no note of discord."— *The Pittsburgh Post.*

THE MACMILLAN COMPANY

Publishers   64–66 Fifth Avenue   New York

The Story of a Round-House and Other Poems *New and Revised Edition*

Cloth, 12mo, $1.30; leather, $1.50.

"John Masefield has produced the finest literature of the year."—*J. M. Barrie.*

"John Masefield is the most interesting poetic personality of the day."—*The Continent.*

"Ah! the story of that rounding the Horn! Never in prose has the sea been so tremendously described."—*Chicago Evening Post.*

The Everlasting Mercy, and the Widow in the Bye-Street

New and Revised Edition. Cloth, $1.25; leather, $1.50.

"Mr. Masefield comes like a flash of light across contemporary English poetry. And he trails glory where his imagination reveals the substances of life."—*Boston Transcript.*

Salt Water Ballads

Cloth, 12mo, $1.00; leather, $1.50.

No living poet has caught the wild beauty of the sea, and imprisoned it in such haunting verse. John Masefield has done in these poems what many consider his finest work.

THE MACMILLAN COMPANY

Publishers   64–66 Fifth Avenue   New York

A Mainsail Haul

Cloth, 12mo, $1.25; leather, $1.50

As a sailor before the mast Masefield has traveled the world over. Many of the tales in this volume are his own experiences written with the same dramatic fidelity displayed in "Dauber."

The Daffodil Fields *Second Edition*

Cloth, 12mo, $1.25; leather, $1.50.

"Neither in the design nor in the telling did, or could, 'Enoch Arden' come near the artistic truth of 'The Daffodil Fields.'"—*Sir Arthur Quiller-Couch*, Cambridge University.

THE MACMILLAN COMPANY

Publishers   64-66 Fifth Avenue   New York